Guide to Becoming a US Department of Transportation Substance Abuse Professional

LaFonia Seals

Copyright © 2024 – LaFonia Seals

All rights reserved. No part of this book may be used or reproduced in any manner whatsoever without written permission except in the case of brief quotations embodied in critical articles or reviews.

Thank you for buying an authorized edition of this book and for complying with copyright laws by not reproducing, scanning, or distributing any part of it in any form without permission. You are supporting writers and their hard work by doing this.

DISCLAIMER: This-book provides general information and guidance on becoming a US Department of Transportation Substance Abuse Professional. It is important to refer to the latest DOT regulations and official resources for the most accurate and up-to-date information.

Intellectual property of Steadfast Life Counseling and Consulting, LLC

www.steadfastlifecounseling.com

Published in the United States of America

First Printing Edition, 2024

INTRODUCTION

Substance Abuse Professionals (SAPs) are important players in transportation safety. They help to ensure both employee and public safety. These certified professionals assess and guide employees who have violated the Department of Transportation's (DOT) drug and alcohol regulations. Why does this matter? Well, understanding the responsibilities of SAPs is important for anyone who is interested in taking on this role to maintain safety and integrity in transportation systems.

But SAPs do more than just enforce regulations. They also help people struggling with substance abuse. It's important that you understand who SAPs are as well as their qualifications and their role in maintaining a safe, drug-free transportation environment before we move ahead.

So let's get into that.

Substance Abuse Professionals are essential to the DOT, which has strict drug and alcohol testing programs for safety-sensitive employees like drivers, pilots, and railroad workers. They have a definitive regulatory framework for these key personnel and it's important that you are well-versed in its contents.

Regulatory Framework

The DOT's guidelines for substance abuse testing are found in 49 CFR Part 40. As mentioned, these rules apply to employees in safety-sensitive jobs across transportation sectors like aviation, trucking, and railroads. Key aspects of these regulations include the following.

Pre-Employment Testing	Prospective employees must pass drug and alcohol tests before starting safety-sensitive jobs.
Random Testing	Employees can be subjected to random drug and alcohol tests.
Post-Accident Testing	After certain accidents, the involved employees must be tested to check for substance abuse.
Reasonable Suspicion Testing	If a supervisor suspects an employee is under the influence, that employee will be required to undergo testing.
Return-to-Duty Testing	Employees who violate substance abuse regulations must be evaluated by an SAP and pass a test before returning to work.

Table 1: Reasons for Testing

Role of Substance Abuse Professionals (SAPs)

SAPs, as you'll come to learn, aren't just rule-enforcers but that doesn't change the fact that they need to ensure compliance with DOT substance abuse testing regulations. This is how they do that.

Assessments	SAPs evaluate employees who violate substance abuse regulations.
Referral for Treatment	Based on their assessments, SAPs refer employees to treatment programs.
Follow-Up Testing Oversight	SAPs monitor an employee's progress during treatment and oversee any follow-up testing that might be needed.
Documentation and Reporting	SAPs maintain detailed records and report their findings to employers as well as the relevant authorities.
Advocates for Safety	SAPs ensure both employee wellness and public safety by making sure that employees are fit for duty before returning to safety-sensitive positions.

Table 2: Responsibilities of the SAP

Scope and Responsibilities

Let's talk about these responsibilities in broader detail now. With all of that said, it's important to note that the duties of SAPs go beyond standard counseling. They are also responsible for conducting thorough assessments as well as creating treatment plans and overseeing the completion of possible rehabilitation programs. Additionally, SAPs act as intermediaries between employees, employers, and the DOT by ensuring that there is clear communication and strict adherence to regulations.

Keep in mind that, as SAPs, you will take on a serious role in ensuring the safety and integrity of the transportation industry. Your work will go far beyond following regulations because you will essentially be the support beneath the framework of public safety. Also important to remember is the fact that SAPs work closely with employers, treatment providers, and regulatory bodies, which means you'll be tasked with making sure that employees get the resources they need instead of just being tossed out on their ears. This collaboration is what strengthens the effectiveness of substance abuse prevention programs.

Now that you understand this a little more clearly, we can move on to the parameters involved in actually stepping into this role.

Table of Contents

Introduction iii
    Regulatory Framework iv
    Role of Substance Abuse Professionals (SAPs) iv
    Scope and Responsibilities v

Chapter 1 – Understanding DOT Regulations 9
    Key Regulations for Substance Abuse Professionals (SAPs) 10
    Compliance Requirements 10

Chapter 2 – Educational Requirements 12
    Educational Requirements for SAPs 12
    Continuing Education and Professional Development 15

Chapter 3 – Gaining Relevant Experience 16
    Building a Strong Foundation in Substance Abuse Counseling 17

Chapter 4 – Professional Networking 19
    The Value of Professional Networking 19
    Leveraging Technology for Networking 21

Chapter 5 – Certification Process 23
    Step-by-Step Guide to Obtaining SAP Certification 23
    Exam Preparation Tips 25

Chapter 6 – Ethical Considerations 26
    Understanding the Ethical Responsibilities of SAPs 26
    Maintaining Confidentiality and Privacy 27

Handling Challenging Situations with Integrity 28

Chapter 7 – Interpersonal Skills & Communication **29**

Building Rapport with Clients and Stakeholders 30

Conflict Resolution and Crisis Intervention Techniques 30

Chapter 8 – Technology in Substance Abuse Counseling **32**

Integrating Technology into the SAP Role 32

Utilizing Digital Tools for Assessments and Monitoring 33

Chapter 9 – Looking at Case Studies **35**

Lessons Learned from Successful Cases 38

Analyzing Challenging Scenarios and Solutions 39

Bonus – FAQs **41**
In Closing **44**
List of Tables **45**
References & Resources **46**

LAFONIA SEALS

Guide to Becoming a US Department of Transportation Substance Abuse Professional

Chapter 1 – Understanding DOT Regulations

As we've already mentioned in the Introduction, the Department of Transportation (DOT) has put strong drug and alcohol testing programs in place in order to maintain safety across the transportation industry. You'll likely remember that the DOT's drug and alcohol testing programs include several types of tests. These are **pre-employment, random, post-accident, reasonable suspicion, return-to-duty**, and **follow-up testing**. As an SAP, you must understand the details of each type of testing in order for you to carry out your responsibilities effectively.

With this said, let's begin with some of the key regulations for SAPs.

Key Regulations for Substance Abuse Professionals (SAPs)

Remember that these rules are primarily laid out in 49 CFR Part 40 and we strongly recommend that you familiarize yourself with the document. It sets the standards for drug and alcohol testing and defines the responsibilities and qualifications for SAPs. Other than the regulations and responsibilities, important points in that document include:

- **The required qualifications and training for SAPs.**
- **Guidelines for referring employees to treatment programs.**
- **SAPs' role in monitoring during the recovery process.**

Making sure that employees adhere to these regulations is necessary. This is important from both a legal standpoint and in ensuring the effectiveness of the DOT's substance abuse prevention efforts. So, what are the compliance requirements?

Compliance Requirements

For SAPs to perform their duties effectively, strict compliance with regulations is a must. This includes staying updated on any changes as well as maintaining confidentiality, conducting assessments fairly, and thoroughly documenting all actions taken. Not only this, but they also need to stay on top of the results of said actions. They have to properly document everything with an unbiased view when reporting. That is the only way to ensure compliance that is fair and to protect the integrity of the program. This brings us to the point of ethics. SAPs must also be mindful of the ethical and legal consequences of their work, but we'll look at that in further detail a little later on.

Essentially, understanding the DOT's drug and alcohol testing programs as well as the regulations that govern SAPs and the compliance requirements are necessary for success in this field. We'll break all of this down in further detail as we progress.

Chapter 2 – Educational Requirements

Becoming an SAP with the United States Department of Transportation requires that you have a strong educational background and a commitment to ongoing professional growth. This is not a job that can be taken lightly and you have to be certain of what you're getting yourself into. When all is said and done, these are people's lives and livelihoods that are at stake. Having the mental fortitude and the qualifications to match will be paramount. With that in mind, we can begin with the educational requirements for SAPs.

Educational Requirements for SAPs

One of the core requirements for becoming an SAP is having the appropriate educational background. The DOT outlines specific qualifications, including requiring a master's or higher degree in a behavioral health-related field. This generally includes areas like counseling, psychology, social work, and other related disciplines. These advanced studies are a prerequisite because the DOT wants to make sure that SAPs have the clinical knowledge necessary for evaluating and addressing substance abuse issues.

Relevant Degrees and Certifications

In addition to a master's degree in a relevant field, there are other certifications that play a role in enhancing an SAP's knowledge and credibility. Certifications from respected organizations, such as the [National Association of Alcoholism and Drug Abuse Counselors](#) (NAADAC) or the [International Certification & Reciprocity Consortium (IC&RC)](#) are great. They showcase an SAP's commitment to upholding high professional standards and staying updated in their field.

Qualifying Credential or License

To qualify as a DOT SAP, you must hold one of the following credentials.

- Nationally certified alcohol/drug abuse counselor through:
    - NAADAC/NCC AP – NCAC I, NCAC II, or MAC national credentials.
    - International Certification & Reciprocity Consortium (IC&RC) – ICADC or ICAADC national credentials.
    - National Board of Certified Counselors (NBCC) – MAC national credential.

- Licensed physician (MD or DO).

- Licensed or certified psychologist.

- Licensed or certified social worker.

- Licensed or certified employee assistance professional.

- Licensed or certified marriage and family therapist.

It's important to know that state-specific credentials or licenses for substance abuse counselors are generally not accepted. It has to be one of the credentials on the list that you have just gone over.

Academic Qualifications

Of course, you already know that SAPs are expected to have a thorough understanding of substance abuse assessment and treatment. This is why completing coursework in addiction counseling, psychotherapy, and behavioral health is so vital. These qualifications equip SAPs with the skills needed to effectively evaluate and support people working in safety-sensitive roles. Essentially, this type of strong academic background is what helps SAPs to navigate the challenges of working with employees who are facing substance abuse issues.

Training

Then there is training. To qualify as a DOT SAP, you must complete 12 hours of professional development that is relevant to SAP duties. This has to be done every three years. Other than that, you would also need to pass a validated exam from a nationally recognized training or professional organization. Remember that training can always be obtained through NAADAC's SAP qualification (or re-qualification) courses. These are typically offered through independent study or live virtual sessions. For more information, visit [SAP Independent Study Course (naadac.org)](naadac.org).

The field is always evolving and that's why continuing your education is so important.

Continuing Education and Professional Development

This reminds us of an old saying: "The only thing constant is change." And those words are so true when it comes to this profession. With new research, treatment methods, and regulatory updates, you have to stay informed to maintain the high level of expertise that will be required of you as an SAP. Ongoing education will help you provide accurate and effective assessments, which is why the DOT requires SAPs to prioritize their professional development to stay current with the latest industry trends.

In the long run, becoming an excellent Substance Abuse Professional requires that you have a strong educational foundation that is bolstered by the relevant certifications and your own dedication to continuous learning.

Chapter 3 –
Gaining Relevant Experience

One thing is for certain. This role requires more than just academic qualifications. You have to gain practical experience to complement your qualifications. It, therefore, goes without saying that you'll need to get up to speed on the practical skills required for the role and how to use various training modalities to build a strong foundation in substance abuse counseling.

The reason for this is that, while a formal education provides a solid understanding of substance abuse counseling, practical experience is where that knowledge is applied. Gaining hands-on experience helps aspiring SAPs develop the skills that they need as well as the sense of judgment and interpersonal understanding that they'll have to use when they're handling real-world situations. This experience is necessary in preparing SAPs to face the challenges they may encounter in the field. But, of course, it becomes a bit like a dog chasing its own tail. In order to be a great SAP, you need experience, but it can be hard to find fieldwork without the experience.

So, what's the solution?

Internships and on-the-job training are excellent ways to bridge that gap between academic learning and practical experience. The best part of this is that working under the guidance of experienced professionals (especially in settings that align with DOT regulations) will give you valuable exposure to diverse cases. It will also enhance your clinical skills.

We recommend that you look for opportunities in clinics and rehabilitation centers or even in organizations that specialize in substance abuse counseling. Many universities and counseling programs also offer supervised internships that provide exposure to various aspects of the field. The goal here is to build a well-rounded skill set.

Building a Strong Foundation in Substance Abuse Counseling

Beyond all of this learning, building a solid foundation in substance abuse counseling involves actively engaging in the field. As such, networking can prove incredibly worthwhile. Connect with professionals in the substance abuse counseling community. Try to attend conferences and workshops, and sign up for webinars and seminars if you can. That way, you'll get to learn from experienced practitioners and expand your network. Just so you know, not all of these have to cost a small fortune. There are a lot of free events.

You can also try to seek out supervision from seasoned professionals who can offer guidance, feedback, and mentorship. Supervision is how you'll refine your clinical skills and develop your approach to counseling. Just be sure to position yourself to work with a variety of cases, including different substances. If you come across opportunities to tap into different cultural backgrounds, grab the opportunity with open arms. Also, look into working on cases where co-occurring disorders are present. This diversity will help to broaden your understanding and it will prepare you to meet the unique needs of employees in safety-sensitive roles.

Last but most certainly not least, keep up with the latest research. You'll want to be at the cutting edge of treatment methods and regulatory updates in the field. To do this, read relevant journals and join online forums. This is how you can continue learning and staying current.

At the end of the day, gaining real-world experience is essential to becoming a skilled Substance Abuse Professional.

Chapter 4 – Professional Networking

Now, let's talk about professional networking. We've already introduced you to this concept in the previous chapter, but it's imperative that we unpack it in broader detail now. Building connections with others in the industry is important because it not only broadens your knowledge but also creates a collaborative environment where you can share in the insights and best practices of those around you and vice versa.

Of course, there is far more value in it than just that alone.

The Value of Professional Networking

Networking is important from both a personal and professional growth front. For SAPs, establishing these connections in the field, as we mentioned, creates a strong support system and opens doors to continuous learning. By networking, you get to stay informed about trends, regulatory updates, and new practices that can enhance your role. Yes, there are some things that you might know, which others don't. However, there is also the possibility that others will know things that you don't It's an all-round win-win. Not only that, but it's a practical way to ensure that you're always up to date and can exchange ideas with others who might be facing similar challenges.

So, how do you do this?

Connecting with Other SAPs

Forming relationships with fellow SAPs can offer you incredible benefits. By sharing experiences and discussing difficult cases, you will contribute to a shared pool of resources within the SAP community. Online forums, social media, and even professional events are great ways to start connecting with other SAPs. Building these relationships will help you grow as a professional and they'll also add valuable perspectives to your practice.

Joining Associations and Organizations

Being part of professional associations can expand your network and keep you engaged with the latest developments in the field. Organizations like the [Employee Assistance Professionals Association (EAPA)](#) and the [National Association of Addiction Treatment Providers (NAATP)](#) both offer valuable opportunities for networking and also for professional growth. Joining these groups will give you access to resources as well as learning opportunities and a platform for connecting with other professionals in substance abuse counseling.

Attending Conferences and Workshops

As mentioned in the previous chapter, conferences and workshops are excellent ways to deepen your knowledge. They're also great places to meet experts in the field and network with others who share your dedication to substance abuse counseling. Participating in these events will give you the opportunity to learn about the latest advancements. Ultimately, the interactions you have can lead to lasting professional connections. We recommend always choosing events that fall in line with your career goals and objectives. Look for industry-specific sectors that can boost your visibility in the industry.

Leveraging Technology for Networking

We're going to discuss technology as part of the SAP role shortly, but it's wise for us to touch on it from a networking standpoint. You might have already guessed it, but technology makes networking easier and more accessible than ever. Online forums and virtual events, for example, present SAPs with many ways to stay connected with other professionals without being in the same room.

One thing that's important to note is that networking isn't just about celebrating successes and socializing. It's also a valuable resource when you're facing challenges. Your professional network can and should provide the support and advice you need when times are tough.

In short, professional networking is a relevant part of being a Substance Abuse Professional. By joining relevant associations and attending conferences, you can build a strong network that supports your growth and success in your role within the DOT.

Networking helps you stay informed and gives you what you need to find guidance when the time calls for it.

Chapter 5 – Certification Process

Once you have the relevant educational background and experience, you can move on to the certification process. This chapter will guide you through the process, including the required documentation and the application process. It's also chock-full of tips for preparing for the certification exam. But before diving into the details, it's important to understand one thing. By passing a certification exam, you assure the DOT that you have the skills and knowledge needed to support their substance abuse prevention program.

Now, how do you obtain SAP certification?

Step-by-Step Guide to Obtaining SAP Certification

To make this process as easy as possible for you, we've created a step-by-step guide on how to get that all-important certification. Some of the steps may already be familiar to you as they were covered in earlier chapters. Still, it's important for us to recap in order to give you an overview of the entire process.

Step 1: Meet Educational Requirements

You'll need a master's or higher degree in a behavioral health-related field, such as counseling, psychology, or social work.

Step 2: Gain Relevant Experience

This can include internships, on-the-job training, or supervised work in substance abuse counseling.

Step 3: Documentation and Application Process

Collect the necessary documents, such as transcripts, proof of your degree, and records of relevant experience. You'll need to submit a complete application to the certifying body. Be thorough because your credentials will be carefully reviewed.

Step 4: Examination

Once your application is approved, you can take the SAP certification exam. This test will cover substance abuse counseling, DOT regulations, and SAP responsibilities. The certifying body will provide details about the exam format, duration, and passing requirements.

Now, there is often confusion as to what the required documentation includes. At the time of writing this, the following documents are acceptable in the application process.

- Copies of your academic transcripts.
- Proof of your master's degree or higher in a relevant field.
- Records of your experience in substance abuse counseling.

- Additional certifications (if applicable).
- A complete and accurate application.

Submit these materials according to the certifying body's instructions. Just be sure to pay attention to deadlines and submission guidelines to avoid any delays. You'll be provided with your examination date and it's important not to miss it!

Exam Preparation Tips

The SAP certification exam tests your knowledge of substance abuse counseling and DOT regulations. To prepare, make sure that you review the study materials provided by the certifying body. In addition to this, familiarize yourself with DOT regulations on substance abuse testing.

If you find that you're having a tough time studying, consider joining study groups or participating in online forums for additional insights. You can also collectively take practice exams to gauge your individual and collective readiness for the exam. This will also help you identify areas where you may need to brush up some more. If you do this, you'll be able to walk into the exam with the confidence that your education and practical experience have prepared you well.

The important takeaway here is that getting SAP certified requires careful preparation, proper documentation, and attention to detail. By following this step-by-step guide, you'll be well-equipped to complete the process and become a certified SAP.

Chapter 6 – Ethical Considerations

Once you have the certification, your efforts won't just stop there. There are also strict ethical standards that you need to adhere to. Remember, these are real people who may be experiencing very serious problems that have led to their substance abuse issues. As such, there are ethical considerations that go far beyond the regulatory framework. This chapter will discuss how you can handle challenging situations with integrity while ensuring privacy is maintained.

Understanding the Ethical Responsibilities of SAPs

As we said above, ethics play a central role in the duties of an SAP. This is because SAPs handle sensitive information about individuals in safety-sensitive positions. Because of that, the decisions that you make in this role can greatly impact both the careers and personal lives of the employees in question.

There are a few ethical responsibilities that serve as the foundation for all of this, so let's unpack them now.

Impartiality	SAPs must remain neutral and objective. They must offer assessments and recommendations without bias.
Cultural Competence	It's essential to respect and understand the diverse backgrounds and beliefs of the employees who are seeking assistance.
Informed Consent	Ensure employees are fully informed about the assessment and treatment process. This should include any consequences of recommendations.
Advocacy	While keeping public safety in mind, SAPs should advocate for the well-being of individuals. They should support both the person and the integrity of the transportation industry.

Table 3: Ethical Role of an SAP

This, of course, all ties into the confidentiality and privacy of the employees in question.

Maintaining Confidentiality and Privacy

Confidentiality is at the core of ethical substance abuse counseling. As an SAP, one of the most important ethics to adhere to is the prioritization of the privacy of those undergoing assessment and treatment.

You will need to follow the Health Insurance Portability and Accountability Act (HIPAA) regulations to protect the privacy and security of health information.

But it's equally important to note that you are bound to offer only limited disclosure to relevant third parties. What that means is that you can only share information with those who have a legitimate need to know certain things as required by DOT regulations. This could include employers.

That also means that you will need to take extra care of how you keep all of that information. Yes, you'll have to maintain accurate records, but you'll also have to ensure that they are securely stored to prevent unauthorized access. This all goes hand in hand with how you'll handle actual field work and challenging situations because that integrity will seep into all of your work.

Handling Challenging Situations with Integrity

Throughout their work, SAPs will undoubtedly encounter difficult situations that require careful ethical decision-making. Some of these challenges include conflicts of interest. To get around this, you would need to do your best to ensure that any personal or professional relationships do not interfere with your ability to make impartial decisions.

You'll also need to manage dual relationships. To do this, you must manage multiple roles carefully to avoid conflicts that could affect your ethical practice.

Finally, you'll need to respect the autonomy of people who may resist assessment or treatment recommendations. What's more, you must handle these situations with care and professionalism.

If you undergo a certification process, you might find topics of this nature. That is because certifying bodies often include ethics-related topics in the certification exam to ensure that all candidates fully understand their responsibilities. Ultimately, by upholding these responsibilities, safeguarding confidentiality, and navigating challenges with integrity, you'll help to maintain the effectiveness of the substance abuse prevention program.

Chapter 7 – Interpersonal Skills & Communication

Becoming a skilled SAP requires not only a solid foundation in substance abuse counseling but also a really strong set of interpersonal skills. This includes everything from effective communication to building rapport with clients and intervening in a crisis.

Communication is arguably the most important aspect of them all because the ability to share information clearly, empathetically, and confidently is a must. We would be remiss not to give you key strategies for developing strong communication skills, so here they are.

Active Listening	Focus fully on the speaker, summarize what you've heard, and ask questions to ensure understanding.
Clarity and Simplicity	Avoid jargon and communicate clearly so everyone can understand the information you provide.
Cultural Awareness	Be mindful of cultural differences in communication. Sensitivity to cultural nuances helps build connections.
Empathy	Show empathy by recognizing and validating the emotions of those you work with.

Table 4: How to Communicate Effectively

Building Rapport with Clients and Stakeholders

Whether you're working with employees who are seeking help or collaborating with employers, you need to know how to build rapport. Without it, conversations can wind up feeling forced and awkward.

But building rapport doesn't have to feel painstaking. It all starts with being genuine in your interactions. That's because authenticity helps build trust and credibility.

Just make sure that you always treat everyone with respect. It shouldn't matter what their background is or their personal circumstances. Be reliable and consistent no matter who they are. And be this way in your communication as well as your actions. This predictability makes you feel like a safe space.

Lastly, remember that the name of the game is collaboration. Work alongside clients and stakeholders with a shared sense of responsibility. This type of collaboration strengthens connections and creates a more cooperative environment — one in which conflict resolution is possible.

Conflict Resolution and Crisis Intervention Techniques

As we said, conflict and crisis situations will arise in the SAP role, and this will require skillful handling. First above all else is tackling conflicts by seeking solutions that meet the needs of everyone who is involved. To do this effectively, you need to learn methods to calm tense situations. These are known as de-escalation techniques and they include the use of calming language and empathy. Added to this, you'll need to maintain a calm demeanor.

We would recommend that you develop standard plans for handling crises, including assessing risks, offering support, and coordinating necessary resources. With standard plans, it will be much easier for you to handle each situation because you won't be starting completely from scratch.

Just keep the cultural context of conflicts or crises in mind. Being culturally competent ensures that your intervention is respectful and effective.

Ultimately, continuously developing these skills will help you develop meaningful connections and navigate the difficulties that sometimes come with substance abuse counseling.

Chapter 8 – Technology in Substance Abuse Counseling

Now that you understand the fundamentals, it's time to look toward the future and the future is now! Cliché aside, technology is playing an increasingly important role in the responsibilities of SAPs and the Department of Transportation recognizes this. This is why SAPs are being encouraged to use digital tools for assessments and monitoring amongst other responsibilities.

But how do you integrate technology into the SAP role?

Integrating Technology into the SAP Role

There's no doubt that technology helps make processes more efficient. It improves communication and provides you with more accurate assessments. We recommend using digital platforms to conduct assessments. These tools make data collection easier, improve accuracy, and provide a smoother experience for clients.

For example, you could utilize telehealth for remote assessments and counseling sessions. This can be especially helpful for employees in remote areas or with limited access to in-person services.

Of course, switching to electronic recordkeeping systems will help you ensure secure, organized, and accessible documentation that can be shared with all of the relevant parties when needed.

Utilizing Digital Tools for Assessments and Monitoring

As stated earlier, various digital tools can improve the assessment and monitoring process in substance abuse counseling. You could use biometric devices to track physical indicators. These could provide objective data to support assessments and progress tracking.

You could also recommend mobile apps that help employees manage their recovery, track sobriety, and access resources. If you can find apps that allow for both counselor and employee use, that would be even better.

We'd also recommend collaborating with e-health platforms that provide a full range of resources. Ideally, they should include educational materials, self-help modules, and community support. Head to the References & Resources section at the very end of this book for examples of these tools. But above all this, you'll want to make sure that you're continuously assessing the digital tools you're using by reviewing feedback and staying updated with industry trends and tool updates to ensure they remain effective.

Integrating technology into your work as a Substance Abuse Professional can truly enhance the efficiency and effectiveness of your role. We would definitely encourage you to continue exploring new tools and assets that you can integrate into your duties.

Chapter 9 – Looking at Case Studies

As our final chapter on becoming an SAP, we're going to look at case studies. These offer valuable examples that can help you connect theory with practice. So, consider the following scenarios.

Case Study 1: Return-to-Duty Success Story

Scenario:
John is a commercial truck driver who tested positive for alcohol during a random DOT test. He was immediately removed from his safety-sensitive duties and referred to a Substance Abuse Professional (SAP). John, who had no previous violations, expressed his willingness to get help. He also expressed that he had been struggling with high levels of stress due to marital problems and financial issues.

Intervention:
The SAP conducted an initial assessment and recommended a treatment plan that included an outpatient program that was focused on alcohol education and relapse prevention. The SAP also arranged follow-up counseling sessions to address stress

management and healthier coping mechanisms. Over the course of treatment, John complied with all the requirements. He attended therapy regularly and remained sober. He realized that potentially losing his job could lead to further stress and financial woes and took the initiative to follow the steps outlined in his program.

Outcome:
After completing the treatment plan and successfully passing the return-to-duty test, John was cleared by the SAP to return to work. The SAP continued follow-up monitoring for one year, during which John maintained sobriety and resumed his duties without further issues. This case highlights the importance of early intervention. Without this type of tailored treatment early on, this may not have been the outcome. Sustained support in achieving long-term recovery led to successful reintegration into the workforce.

Case Study 2: Cultural Competence in Action

Scenario:
Maria is a transit employee who was referred to a SAP after testing positive for marijuana. During the initial assessment, it became clear that cultural and familial expectations played a significant role in her substance use. Maria explained that marijuana was commonly used during family gatherings, and she hadn't recognized its potential impact on her safety-sensitive role.

Intervention:
The SAP, who had experience working with diverse populations, utilized culturally competent techniques to address Maria's situation. The SAP engaged in open, non-judgmental conversations about her cultural influences. By incorporating these factors into the treatment plan, the SAP helped Maria understand how

substance use could affect her career and safety while respecting her cultural background.

Outcome:
Maria completed a treatment program that focused on substance use education and developing boundaries for family events. She passed the follow-up tests and was allowed to return to work. The SAP's cultural competence was vital in handling this case. This shows how understanding cultural dynamics can lead to better outcomes.

Case Study 3: Addressing Resistance to Treatment

Scenario:
Mike is an aviation mechanic who was referred to an SAP after failing a random drug test for opioids. Although prescribed for a legitimate injury, Mike had exceeded the prescribed dosage, which led to dependency. Initially, Mike was resistant to the idea of treatment. He believed that his use was justified because of his injury.

Intervention:
The SAP employed motivational interviewing techniques to address Mike's reluctance. By asking open-ended questions and listening empathetically, the SAP helped Mike recognize the risks associated with his opioid use, especially in a safety-sensitive role. Gradually, Mike became more open to the idea of treatment. He acknowledged the potential impact of his substance use on his work and safety.

Outcome:
The SAP referred Mike to a pain management specialist and an addiction counselor. Through this coordinated approach, Mike received the appropriate medical treatment for his pain while

addressing his dependency. After completing his treatment, Mike passed his return-to-duty test and continued to receive follow-up monitoring for six months. This case demonstrates how patient and empathetic interventions can help overcome initial resistance and lead to positive outcomes.

What can we learn from all of this?

Lessons Learned from Successful Cases

One of the main takeaways from the various cases is the significance of individualized, client-centered approaches. Tailoring interventions to meet the unique needs and circumstances of each individual proves to be highly effective. In cases where strategies were customized to address specific issues, the results were notably positive. This goes to show that a one-size-fits-all approach rarely works in this field.

Another essential element of success lies in building trust and rapport between the SAP and the individual seeking assistance. The outcomes of many interventions often hinge on the level of trust established. Strong communication and relationship-building are a must as you could see from Mike's case.

Collaboration with stakeholders, including employers, treatment providers, and other relevant parties, is equally important. In cases where multiple parties worked together, the coordinated efforts saw to it that the individual in question received the comprehensive support that they needed for recovery and reintegration. These collaborations allowed for a more holistic approach. In the end, this addressed not only substance abuse but also any underlying issues that might impact the individual's long-term success.

Analyzing Challenging Scenarios and Solutions

When it comes to analyzing challenging scenarios, navigating difficult situations is part of the SAP role. For instance, resistance to treatment is a common issue, but many successful cases highlight strategies that can engage resistant clients and motivate them to embrace positive change. SAPs have found that patience, empathy, and motivational interviewing can often break through initial barriers and encourage clients to commit to the treatment process.

Legal and ethical dilemmas are another challenge that SAPs frequently encounter. Successful cases show that staying within regulatory guidelines and upholding ethical standards are key when navigating these complex situations. SAPs must often balance the needs of the individual with legal obligations to ensure that the integrity of the process is maintained. Moreover, they must do this without compromising their ethical principles.

In cases where individuals present with both substance use and mental health disorders, effective strategies for managing co-occurring disorders are non-negotiable. Successful interventions often involve a coordinated approach in which an SAP has to work closely with mental health professionals to ensure that both aspects of the individual's condition are addressed simultaneously. This integrated care model is essential for long-term recovery because it provides a more comprehensive solution to the challenges of the person in question.

Examining these scenarios and solutions allows you, as a current or aspirant SAP, to continue refining your approaches and enhancing your effectiveness in the field.

Bonus – FAQs

You've reached the end of this guide, but we'd like to provide you with a quick reference area in the form of frequently asked questions.

Here, we'll answer the most common questions from individuals looking to become SAPs. So, whether you're curious about educational requirements or the certification process, you'll find clear guidance to help you pursue this rewarding career.

1. What are the main requirements to become an SAP with the Department of Transportation?

To become an SAP, you'll need a master's degree in a behavioral health-related field (like counseling or social work), along with relevant experience in substance abuse counseling. Additionally, you'll need to complete the SAP certification process, which includes training and passing a certification exam.

2. What does the certification process involve?

The certification process requires you to complete a specific training program, pass an exam, and submit documentation of your qualifications. You'll also need to keep your certification up to date by completing continuing education requirements.

3. Are there any ethical concerns I need to be aware of as a SAP?

Yes, SAPs must follow strict ethical guidelines. You'll need to remain impartial in your assessments and maintain confidentiality at all times. It's also important to navigate legal and ethical dilemmas carefully while adhering to Department of Transportation regulations.

4. What resources are available to help me learn more about becoming a SAP?

There are plenty of resources available to guide you on your journey. Books, articles, websites, and organizations like the National Association of Addiction Treatment Providers (NAATP) can provide valuable information. Additionally, you can find courses and seminars that offer deeper insights into the field.

5. How can I connect with mentors or other experienced SAPs?

Connecting with experienced professionals is a great way to get advice and support. You can attend conferences, join professional associations, or reach out through networking platforms like LinkedIn to find mentors who can guide you through the challenges of becoming a SAP.

6. What should I do when I face challenging cases or ethical dilemmas?

When you're dealing with a tough case, seeking guidance from a mentor or experienced SAP can be incredibly helpful. It's important to have a network of professionals you can turn to for advice when complex situations arise.

7. How can I stay updated on changes in DOT regulations?

Staying informed about regulatory changes is crucial. You can subscribe to newsletters from the Department of Transportation, join professional organizations, and attend relevant workshops or seminars to ensure you're up to date on the latest requirements.

8. How can I benefit from participating in online communities and forums?

Online communities and forums are great places to connect with other SAPs and share your experiences. You can gain new perspectives, ask for advice, and stay informed about trends and challenges in the field. It's also a convenient way to network with peers from across the country.

In Closing

As you work toward becoming a Substance Abuse Professional (SAP), staying informed and continuing to learn will help you reach the level of success that you've been hoping for. Just remember that this role is important in helping keep people alive in safety-sensitive jobs. Also, take comfort in the fact that you're not alone. There are plenty of resources and people to help you along the way.

LIST OF TABLES

Table 1: Reasons for Testing iv
Table 2: Responsibilities of the SAP iv
Table 3: Ethical Role of an SAP 27
Table 4: How to Communicate Effectively 29

References & Resources

- **Substance Abuse and Mental Health Services Administration (SAMHSA)**
  Website: https://www.samhsa.gov
  SAMHSA provides extensive information on substance use, treatment resources, and guidelines for professionals.

- **National Institute on Drug Abuse (NIDA)**
  Website: https://www.drugabuse.gov
  NIDA offers research-based information on substance use and its effects, treatment options, and guidelines for counselors.

- **Department of Transportation (DOT) Office of Drug and Alcohol Policy and Compliance**
  Website: https://www.transportation.gov/odapc
  DOT's website provides detailed information on the drug and alcohol testing regulations for SAPs, including 49 CFR Part 40.

- **National Association of Alcoholism and Drug Abuse Counselors (NAADAC)**
  Website: https://www.naadac.org
  NAADAC offers certifications, training, and educational resources for substance abuse professionals.

- **International Certification & Reciprocity Consortium (IC&RC)**
  Website: https://www.internationalcredentialing.org
  IC&RC provides certifications and guidelines for professionals working in addiction counseling and prevention.

- **Health Insurance Portability and Accountability Act (HIPAA) Regulations**
  Website: https://www.hhs.gov/hipaa/index.html
  HIPAA is critical for understanding privacy and confidentiality requirements for SAPs working in the healthcare field.

- **American Society of Addiction Medicine (ASAM)**
  Website: https://www.asam.org
  ASAM offers guidelines, publications, and research related to substance abuse treatment and addiction medicine.

- **The Employee Assistance Professionals Association (EAPA)**
  Website: https://www.eapassn.org
  EAPA provides resources for professionals working in employee assistance programs, including those related to substance abuse counseling.

- **National Association of Addiction Treatment Providers (NAATP)**
  Website: https://www.naatp.org
  NAATP offers resources, networking, and education for those working in addiction treatment, including information relevant to SAPs.

- **Journal of Substance Abuse Treatment**
 Website: https://www.journalofsubstanceabusetreatment.com
 A peer-reviewed journal offering research, case studies, and treatment strategies related to substance use disorders.

Mobile Apps for Recovery Management

- **Sober Grid**: A social networking app that connects people in recovery and provides tools for tracking sobriety.

- **Recovery Record**: A user-friendly app that allows individuals and their counselors to track recovery progress, share notes, and monitor sobriety together.

- **I Am Sober**: This app allows users to track their sobriety, journal progress, and connect with a community for support.

E-Health Platforms

- **Talkspace** or **BetterHelp**: These platforms offer online counseling services and can be a valuable resource for employees who need remote access to licensed professionals.

- **Pear Therapeutics**: A digital health platform offering tools for managing addiction, including apps that incorporate evidence-based therapies.

- **SMART Recovery**: This platform provides self-help resources, online meetings, and educational materials for individuals managing their recovery.

www.ingramcontent.com/pod-product-compliance
Lightning Source LLC
Chambersburg PA
CBHW052034030426
42337CB00027B/5002